Where am I?

Bobbie Kalman

🌳 Crabtree Publishing Company

www.crabtreebooks.com

Created by Bobbie Kalman

Author and Editor-in-Chief
Bobbie Kalman

Educational consultants
Reagan Miller
Joan King
Elaine Hurst

Editors
Joan King
Reagan Miller
Kathy Middleton

Proofreader
Crystal Sikkens

Photo research
Bobbie Kalman

Design
Bobbie Kalman
Katherine Berti

Production coordinator
Katherine Berti

Prepress technician
Katherine Berti

Photographs
BigStockPhoto: p. 15 (top right)
Circa Art: p. 16 (bottom)
Digital Stock: p. 7
iStockphoto: p. 4
Shutterstock: cover, p. 1, 3, 5, 6, 8, 9,
    10, 11, 12, 13, 15 (except top right)

Library and Archives Canada Cataloguing in Publication

Kalman, Bobbie, 1947-
    Where am I? / Bobbie Kalman.

(My world)
ISBN 978-0-7787-9437-0 (bound).--ISBN 978-0-7787-9481-3 (pbk.)

1. Geography--Juvenile literature. 2. Geography--Terminology--
Juvenile literature. I. Title. II. Series: My world (St. Catharines, Ont.)

G133.K34 2010   j910   C2009-906070-1

Library of Congress Cataloging-in-Publication Data

Kalman, Bobbie.
    Where am I? / Bobbie Kalman.
        p. cm. -- (My world)
    ISBN 978-0-7787-9481-3 (pbk. : alk. paper) -- ISBN 978-0-7787-9437-0
(reinforced library binding : alk. paper)
    1. Geography--Juvenile literature. I. Title. II. Series.

    G133.K254 2010
    910--dc22

                                                    2009041187

Crabtree Publishing Company
www.crabtreebooks.com   1-800-387-7650

Printed in China/122009/CT20091009

Published in Canada
Crabtree Publishing
616 Welland Ave.
St. Catharines, Ontario
L2M 5V6

Published in the United States
Crabtree Publishing
PMB 59051
350 Fifth Avenue, 59th Floor
New York, New York 10118

Published in the United Kingdom
Crabtree Publishing
Maritime House
Basin Road North, Hove
BN41 1WR

Published in Australia
Crabtree Publishing
386 Mt. Alexander Rd.
Ascot Vale (Melbourne)
VIC 3032

Words to know

beach

canyon

cave

cliff

desert

island

mountain

plain

ocean

wave

Land has different shapes.

In some places, the land is flat.

In other places, the land is high.

The different shapes of land
are called **landforms**.

Where am I?

High, rocky landforms are all around me.

They are called **mountains**.

I am sitting on a mountain with my friend.

We climbed all the way up here!

I am on a flat field with no trees.

The field has grasses and flowers.

Where am I?

I am on a **plain**.

I am in a dry place.

It does not rain a lot here.

Where am I?

I am in a **desert**.

I am in a dark place
under a big rock.
It looks like a room.
Where am I?
I am in a **cave**.

8

I am in salty water.

The water is full of **waves**.

Where am I?

I am in an **ocean**.

A big wave is chasing me!

I am beside an ocean.

The land is sandy and flat.

Where am I?

I am on a **beach**.

There is water all around this landform.

Where am I?

I am on an **island**.

island

I am sitting on a tall rock above the ocean.
Where am I?
I am on a **cliff** with my sister.

cliff

There are tall rocks all around.

There is a deep hole behind me.

Where am I?

I am in a **canyon** with my mother.

Which children are:

1. in a cave
2. on a mountain
3. in a canyon
4. on a cliff
5. in the ocean

Notes for adults

What are landforms?

Landforms are the shapes of land on Earth. *Where am I?* introduces children to some of Earth's landforms, such as mountains, caves, beaches, cliffs, deserts, and more. Children are given picture and word clues to guess where the child in the picture is.

What are nearby landforms?

Which of the landforms shown in this book are near where the children live? Ask them to look at the picture the girl on page 4 is painting and ask which landform they think is in the picture. What else can they see in the picture (grass, flowers, water, sun, and houses)? Ask the children to look at how the land looks on their way home from school. Are there flat areas with flowers? Are there high areas? Are there areas of water? Ask them to draw a picture of what they have seen.

Landforms through art

There are many artists who paint landscapes. Find some landscape art books in the library and introduce children to landforms through art. Ask them to practice painting some landscapes. Then take a field trip and have them paint the landscapes as they really are.

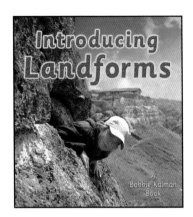

Introducing Landforms shows Earth's continents and oceans and many landforms that make Earth a beautiful work of art.

Cliff Walk at Pourville by Claude Monet